First published 1982
Second impression 1983
The Hamlyn Publishing Group Limited
London · New York · Sydney · Toronto
Astronaut House, Feltham, Middlesex, England

ISBN 0 600 36674 X
Printed in Italy

The Lonely House

Sally Sheringham

Illustrated by Douglas Hall

Hamlyn

London · New York · Sydney · Toronto

Contents

The House gets some bad news

Once upon a time (before you or I or even our great-uncles were born), behind rusty gates and a garden that looked like a wild tangly jungle, stood a big dark house.

Once it had been a fine, grand house, but now it was very old; its walls were crumbling and it had lost all its paint. Dusty cobwebs hung in every room, and its windows were so grimy that it could barely see out of them. Its floorboards were rotting and there was a hole in the roof, through which the rain came in.

It was a house that had seen better days.

Poor old house.

But the saddest thing of all was that nobody lived in it – not even a beetle, or a spider.

The last spider had moved out years ago. 'Sorry, House, but I'm off to find somewhere more comfortable to live,' it had told him. 'You're far too damp and, besides, because no flies come near you, I'm getting hungry,' and the spider had crawled away.

So the Old House was left all alone, with no one to talk to and no one to care for him. And, to make matters worse, he had two very smart neighbours. On one side was a pretty, pink house with ivy growing up it, and on the other a bright blue house with a gleaming

white front door and clean shiny windows. They both had big families living in them. The Old House would peer enviously out of his grimy windows at his lucky neighbours. How he wished that he was a smartly-painted house with a happy family living in him.

The Pink House and the Blue House were very unkind to their shabby neighbour. 'I'm not surprised no one lives in you, you are so old and ugly,' said the Pink House. 'Why, no one would want to *look* at you, let alone live in you.'

'Yes,' said the Blue House. 'You are a disgrace to the street. If it weren't for you, this would be a smart street – the smartest in town.'

'And I'll tell you something else,' said the Pink House. 'The people who live in me were talking about you. They were saying that the Council were going to pull you down and build a smart new house in your place.'

'Hurray!' said the Blue House.

'Oh, no!' said the Old House. He didn't want to be pulled down and replaced by a smart new house. A large, grubby tear rolled from one of his upstairs windows.

'Perhaps the Pink House was lying,' he thought to himself. But, the very next day, a man from the Council walked through the rusty gates and up the overgrown path.

The Old House stood up as straight as he could, and tried to look as though he were the sort of place where people would want to live.

But it was no use. The man from the Council took one look at him and said, 'Oh deary me.'

He looked inside all the rooms, cobwebs tangling up in his hair and the dust turning his moustache grey. 'Oh deary me,' he said again, stepping on a rotting floorboard. 'No one will ever want to live in you again, and you'll cost far too much to repair. I'm afraid, old chap, that you'll have to be pulled down. I'll send two of my men round after Christmas,' and he made a note of it in a little book.

The Old House was too upset to speak, but the other houses were pleased. 'Hurray!' whispered the Pink House.

'About time, too,' whispered the Blue House.

Norman Monster

At the very moment that the man from the Council was telling the Old House that he would have to be pulled down, a long way away, a monster called Norman was being told off, for the eighty-third time that day, by his mother, Mrs Monster.

'You are a lazy, good-for-nothing, clumsy, greedy, ugly monster,' she was saying.

'Sorry, Mum,' said Norman, shuffling in his monster-sized chair.

'You are far too old to be living with your parents,' continued Mrs Monster. 'Why, all the other monsters of your age went off to make their fortunes years ago. Just my luck to be stuck with a lump of a son like you, who sits around in a comfy chair telling silly jokes and watching his mother and father do all the work. You should be ashamed of yourself.'

Although Norman had heard this said several hundred times before, for the first time he suddenly *did* feel ashamed of himself.

'Okay then, Mum,' he said, standing up and knocking over the chair by mistake, then hitting his head on the ceiling. 'I'm going to seek my fortune – today.'

Mrs Monster's large mouth dropped open. Was this really her son speaking?

Norman kept to his word. After packing his two favourite things – a monster-sized toothbrush and a monster book of jokes – into a red-spotted handkerchief, off he went.

Mr and Mrs Monster waved goodbye at the garden gate.

'Good luck, son,' said Mr Monster. 'Send us a postcard.'

Mrs Monster wiped her eyes with her apron. Even though she was always getting cross with Norman, she still felt sad to see him go.

Norman lumbered off down the street, feeling happier and happier by the minute. He would miss his mother and father, of course, but how lovely it felt to be free, to do exactly what he wanted and have no one to tell him not to. He did a little dance in the street. No one told him not to be silly. 'I *am* enjoying myself,' he thought.

Soon Norman had left Monster Town, and was walking through a huge forest. When he came out on the other side he saw some very strange creatures; they were small, with hair and soft skin. And they wore clothes! They were, of course, people, but Norman, who had never left Monster Town in his life, hadn't seen any before. 'I

wonder what they are,' he thought. 'I think I'll go over to them and say hello.'

And he did. But as soon as the people saw Norman they screamed and ran away.

'I won't hurt you. I'm a friendly monster,' Norman shouted. But the people didn't believe him, and ran even faster.

This happened over and over again. Wherever he went, people would scream and run away. You couldn't really blame them. They'd never seen a monster before, and Norman did look particularly big and frightening and 'monsterish'.

So Norman, feeling very lonely

and rather homesick, spent the night under the stars in a turnip field. 'I'm never going to make any friends,' he thought sadly as he rested his big ugly head on a turnip, 'unless I can prove that I'm a friendly monster.'

Norman slept badly – turnips don't make the most comfortable

of pillows, not even for a monster with a very thick skin – and in the middle of the night, he opened his eyes. To his surprise, a man was standing over him. He was wearing a crooked black hat and had a missing front tooth and a bristly chin. To you or me, he would look the sort of man who couldn't be trusted, but to Norman he was just a friendly person who didn't scream and run away from him.

'Well, monster, how would you like to make your fortune?' asked the man.

Norman blinked. 'Very much,' he said.

'Follow me then,' said the man. So Norman did.

After walking a long way, they came to a fairground.

'Now,' said the man. 'This is how I propose to make both of us very, very rich,' and he told Norman his cunning plan . . .

'Roll up, roll up, ladies and gentlemen, for a glimpse of Norman, the ugliest, most hideous monster in the world,' shouted the man the next morning.

And soon, people were giving him money and then queueing all the way round the edge of the fairground to catch a glimpse of Norman, who stood in a cage behind a curtain in a tent. When the tent was full of people, the man swished back the curtain and the crowd stared, then gasped, then went, 'Oooooh', or 'Errrr', or '*Ugh*'.

And Norman stared back at them, feeling a bit silly and also a bit miserable, for no one, not even an ugly monster, likes people to go

'*Ugh*' at them. 'But although I'm not enjoying myself, at least I'm going to make my fortune,' he thought to himself.

People flocked from far and wide to see Norman.

On Friday, he asked the man with the missing front tooth for his half of the money, which was what they had agreed on.

The man threw back his head

and laughed. 'You don't really think,' he said, 'that I'm going to keep my promise, do you? Why, my plan is that you stay locked up in the cage and I keep all the money.'

Norman became very, very angry. He had been cheated. With a monster roar, and gathering together all his strength, he crashed straight through the bars of the cage and grabbed the man round the throat with his claws.

The man stopped grinning and began to look very frightened. 'Okay, Norman,' he said, eyeing the sharp claws. 'I'll give you half the money.'

Twelve gold crowns. Norman had never seen so much money in his life. He wrapped it up carefully in his spotted handkerchief along with his joke book and his toothbrush, and quickly set on his way.

'Now I have money,' he thought, 'I can do anything. Sail round the world . . . stay in a hotel with my very own private bathroom . . .'

But that was just where Norman was wrong. No hotel wanted a monster as a guest – why, he wouldn't fit into any of the beds. And no boat owner wanted a monster as a passenger – why, the boat would sink straight away.

Poor Norman. No one wanted him. So he walked and walked, along country lanes and in quiet places where he wouldn't meet anyone.

'Oh dear, I'm never going to find somewhere I can live – a place where I'll be wanted,' thought Norman sadly.

And then, one day, he passed the rusty gates of the empty Old House.

'It doesn't look as though anyone's living there,' he thought. 'Maybe, as long as the house doesn't mind, I could stay there for a while,' and he walked through the squeaky gates and up the overgrown path.

The lonely Old House was overjoyed to have a visitor at last. And, even though the visitor was an ugly monster, an ugly monster was far better than no one.

'Stay as long as you like,' said the House, creaking open his front door to let Norman in.

'Oh, thank you, House,' said Norman, happily stepping inside. 'I'm going to like it here. I hope you like jokes. I know hundreds.'

'Was I seeing things or was that a monster that just walked in next door?' said the Pink House.

'Yes, it was,' said the Blue House. 'Whatever next?'

Nigel Mouse

At the very moment that the House was welcoming Norman Monster, a long way away, a mouse called Nigel sat at his easel in the garden, painting a picture of a tulip. He was just painting bright pink petals, when suddenly he spied his old enemy, Wilf Whiskers, peering

at him through the rose bushes.

'Oh, mousetraps,' said Nigel, picking up his easel and stool and paints and scuttling off into the house. 'Can't that cat ever leave me to paint in peace?'

It was always the same – just when Nigel had settled down to paint a piece of cheese, or a sunset, or a blackbird bathing in a puddle, Wilf Whiskers would creep up behind him and so he'd have to stop painting and scuttle away. For Nigel was afraid of Wilf Whiskers; he had sharp claws and, what was more, *he didn't like mice*.

'There's nothing else for it,' Nigel decided, once he was safely back in his hole. 'The only way I'm going to be able to paint in peace and quiet is to move somewhere that doesn't have a cat.'

So he piled up his paints and paper and easel into his little red wheelbarrow, and waited till

nightfall. Then, when he was certain that Wilf Whiskers had gone for his midnight prowl, Nigel set off to find another home.

He walked and walked, huffing and puffing when he pushed the wheelbarrow uphill, and running to keep up with it when he went downhill.

Just as dawn was breaking, Nigel came to a grain store. 'I wouldn't mind living here,' he thought. So he crept in under the door and came face to face with – a large, fat rat!

'Buzz off,' the rat snarled. 'I got here first. And, besides, *I don't like mice.*'

So Nigel buzzed off. The rat was a lot bigger than he was and his teeth looked very sharp.

He walked a little further and came to a farm house. 'I wouldn't mind living here,' he thought. But suddenly, he found himself face to face with – a large, black, farm dog!

'Hop it,' snarled the dog. '*I don't like mice.*'

So Nigel hopped it. The dog was a lot bigger than he was and he had a very fierce face.

Soon Nigel came to a beautiful palace.

'I wouldn't mind living here,' said Nigel, and walked boldly up the drive, through the front door and down long corridors towards the kitchen.

Suddenly, he was being picked up, wheelbarrow and all, by a guard, and carried back down the long corridor. Soon he found himself face to face with – the king himself!

'So, little mouse,' boomed the king. 'You thought you could sneak into my palace, did you? You know something? *I don't like mice.*'

'I'm very sorry, your majesty,' squeaked Nigel. 'You see, I'm looking for a home where I can paint in peace.'

'So you're a painter, eh?' said the king, narrowing his eyes. 'Tell you what. If you paint my portrait, and I'm pleased with it, I'll allow you to make my palace your home.'

'Oh, thank you, your majesty,' said Nigel, mopping his brow before setting up his easel.

But he soon found he had a big problem on his paws. For the king was very, very ugly. He had a big red nose, sticking-out ears, hardly any hair and a large wart on his chin.

The king sat still while Nigel painted. At last it was finished.

'Let me see,' cried the king, eagerly snatching the portrait off

the easel. He looked at it, then let out a long, loud roar.

'This looks nothing like me,' he bellowed. 'It makes me look ugly – *horrible*,' and he tore Nigel's work of art up into tiny pieces. Then he said, 'If you don't get out of my palace now, this instant, you stupid little mouse, I shall set the palace cats on you.'

Nigel packed up his little red wheelbarrow and was out of the palace before you could say 'very ugly king'.

So Nigel was still without a home. For days and days he wandered about looking for some place where he could paint in peace, but everywhere he went he got the same response: '*We don't like mice.*'

He had just about given up hope of ever finding a home, when one day he passed the rusty gates of the Old House. Nigel peered in. How peaceful it looked – and what an unusual garden. Why, it looked more like a jungle than a garden. How he'd love to paint it. He'd love to paint the Old House, too – there weren't many old houses like that left. Come to think of it, he

wouldn't mind living there, either; it didn't look as if it had a cat.

Nervously, Nigel pushed his little red wheelbarrow up the overgrown path. When he reached the front door, he explained his situation to the House.

'You can stay as long as you like, little mouse,' cried the House. One visitor was good, but two were even better, and he creaked open his front door.

Happily, Nigel stepped inside, and came face to face with – Norman Monster! He was just about to run away in fright, but Norman was so friendly that Nigel soon felt at home.

'All sensible houses get rid of mice, not welcome them in,' whispered the Pink House to the Blue House.

Gertrude Ghost

At the very moment that the House and Norman Monster were making Nigel Mouse feel at home, a long way away a ghost called Gertrude was playing a trick on a duchess, who happened to be Lady Winterbottom's most important guest.

Gertrude didn't normally play tricks on Lady Winterbottom's guests. Well, let's say she would have liked to have done, but she wasn't allowed to. However, she was getting very bored with being good the whole time and, besides, she didn't like the duchess at all. She was very snooty, and also she

didn't believe in ghosts. Once, Gertrude had heard her say that only very silly people believed in ghosts, so Gertrude had decided to teach her a lesson.

The duchess was getting dressed for dinner, so when the duchess wasn't looking, Gertrude kept floating out from behind a

curtain and hiding things. She hid the duchess' fan under the clock on the mantelpiece; she hid her high-heeled satin shoes in the four-poster bed; and she hid her diamond necklace in the soap dish.

The duchess got more and more confused. She knew that she hadn't put her fan under the clock or her necklace in the soap dish. But if she hadn't, who had? Her maid wasn't with her, and there was no one else in the room. And where were her shoes? She was sure she'd left them in the bottom of her wardrobe. She sat down on the bed and then got up again in a hurry. Whatever was in her bed? It was her shoes! 'I know I didn't put them in such a silly place,' she said. 'Or did I? Perhaps I'm going mad.'

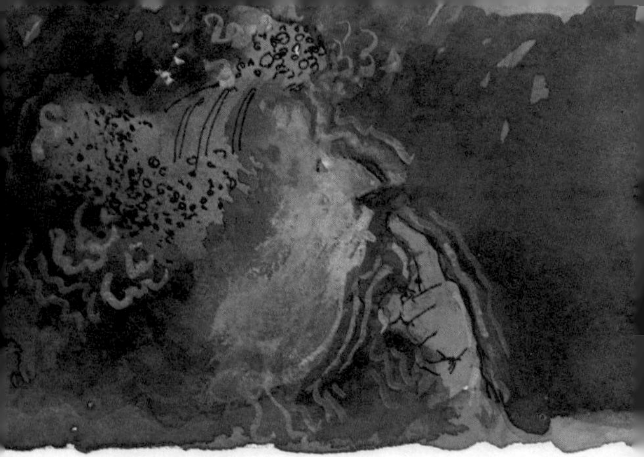

And then, suddenly, the candle blew out.

'Oh, bother,' said the duchess. 'How can I get dressed for dinner in the dark?'

And then, although normally a tough, brave person, she started to tremble like a jelly. For she had seen something white moving

behind the curtain. Could it be a ghost?

'No, it *can't* be,' she said. 'Only silly people believe in ghosts.'

'Oooooooooo,' said Gertrude in her most ghostly voice. 'Then you must be silly, tooooooooo,' and she floated out from behind the curtain.

'EEK! It *is* a ghost,' shrieked the duchess and rushed from the room dressed only in her underwear. Her screams could be heard all over the house.

How Gertrude laughed. That would pay her back for not believing in ghosts. And how hilarious, a

grand duchess turning up for dinner in just her underwear!

The duchess left that night in a huff, saying she'd never return again.

Lady Winterbottom called for Gertrude immediately.

'Now Gertrude,' she said, frowning at her over the top of her glasses. 'The reason you have been allowed to haunt my house for all these years is because you

promised that you wouldn't upset any of my guests. And now you've broken your promise. And it would be the duchess, of all people. Why, she'll tell everyone that my house is haunted, and then no one will want to visit me.'

'I'm very sorry, Lady Winterbottom,' said Gertrude. And she really was. Although she didn't like the duchess, she did like Lady Winterbottom. After all, there weren't many people who allowed a ghost to haunt their house.

'Being sorry isn't enough,' said Lady Winterbottom. 'I'm afraid, Gertrude, that you'll have to find another house to haunt.'

Gertrude pleaded with her to let

her stay, but Lady Winterbottom's mind was made up. So, sadly, Gertrude set off, that very night, to find another house to haunt.

She floated along, not quite flying, but not quite walking, either, the way ghosts do, until she came to a house. 'It's a little small for my taste, but I'll give it a try,' she thought, and floated in through the window. But it was too small. There were no interesting secret places to hide in, no dark corners or attics or long passages. In fact it was a house quite unfit for a ghost!

All the other places Gertrude explored were the same, apart from a hospital, which was nice and big and old, but Gertrude decided that it wouldn't be fair to haunt a hospital. If any of the ill patients saw her they would be frightened and perhaps get worse.

And then she floated past a house that was almost suitable. It was still a bit small, but at least it looked rather ghostly. It was in the middle of a dark wood, from which an owl hooted.

'That'll do nicely, for the time being,' she thought. 'New home, here I come,' and she floated in through the attic window. But whom should she meet but another ghost!

'Er – oh, hello,' said Gertrude, rather embarrassed, for ghosts don't usually mix with other ghosts.

' "*Hello?*" ' said the other ghost. 'Don't you mean "*good-bye*"? I got here first. This is my house and I, and only I, am allowed to haunt it.'

'Oh, all right then,' said Gertrude, and floated back out of the window. 'I'm never going to find a house as good as Lady Winterbottom's,' she thought sadly as she floated along. How she wished she'd never played the trick on the duchess.

And then, suddenly, ahead of her she saw, in the middle of a garden that looked like a jungle, the perfect house to haunt. It was as good as, no, better, far better, than Lady Winterbottom's. For it was older and bigger and darker and more ghostly-looking than any house she'd ever seen before.

She floated up to the front door.

The House was delighted to see Gertrude. 'Have you come to haunt me?' he asked hopefully.

'Er, yes. That is, if you don't mind,' said Gertrude.

'Not at all. Stay for as long as you like,' said the House. Two visitors were good, three were even

better, and he creaked open his front door for her.

Gertrude floated inside, and came face to face with a monster and a mouse.

'Oh good,' said Norman. 'Someone else to listen to my jokes.'

'Oh good,' said Nigel. 'I've always wanted to paint a picture of a ghost.'

Soon Gertrude felt quite at home.

The Pink House and the Blue House looked at each other.

'The Old House has gone mad,' said the Pink House. 'I mean, would you welcome in a ghost?'

'No, I certainly wouldn't,' said the Blue House shuddering.

Primrose Witch

At the very moment that the House, Norman Monster and Nigel Mouse were making Gertrude feel at home, a long way away a very old witch called Primrose sat in her room in the turret of a castle and said, 'Bother' three times.

For, the worst thing that could happen to a witch had happened to Primrose. She had forgotten all her magic spells. She had slowly been forgetting them, one by one, over the years, and now she had forgotten the only one she could remember, which was turning daisies into jam doughnuts.

'I'll have one more go,' sighed Primrose, waving her now un-magic wand, and said, 'Three wasps' wings, two hens' feathers, a mouse's whisker and . . .' Then Primrose stopped and scratched her head. 'Oh, what is it? A lamb chop? No, no. A cheeseburger? No, no. A goose's egg? Yes, let's try that.'

But the daisies stayed as daisies, without a hint of a jam doughnut about them.

'Oh, *bother*,' said Primrose

again. 'Now I really have forgotten every magic spell I knew. I have no right to call myself a witch, for whoever has heard of a witch who has forgotten all her magic spells? I'm too old, that's my trouble,' and a tear ran down her wrinkled cheek.

And then, to make matters even worse, she heard trumpets playing a fanfare. She looked out of the window. As she'd feared, it was the queen returning from her holiday at the seaside in a glass coach.

'Oh, bother,' said Primrose yet again. 'When the queen finds out I've forgotten all my magic, she'll send me away to that horrible Home for Retired Witches.'

Primrose kept her fingers crossed that the queen wouldn't require her services. But, unfortunately, the very next day the queen's maid climbed the stairs to Primrose's room to tell her that the queen wanted to see her straight away. So Primrose dusted her black pointed hat, polished her un-magic wand and then, shaking with fright, followed the maid to the queen's bedroom.

'Ah, Primrose,' said the queen. 'I have decided that this yellow dress doesn't suit me. So I would like you to turn it into a blue dress.'

Primrose gulped. She had forgotten this spell years ago. She would have to pretend.

'Certainly, your majesty,' she said, raising her un-magic wand and muttering, 'Toadstools, cowslips and a horse's shoe, turn the queen's dress from yellow to blue.'

But, as Primrose had expected, the queen's dress remained as yellow as ever.

So Primrose tried again. 'Good-bye, goodnight, good-

morning, hello. This dress must be blue, not yellow.'

But the dress still remained as yellow as ever.

Primrose got into a terrible fluster. Whatever could she do now?

And then the queen said, 'Primrose, I hope you haven't forgotten how to perform magic tricks.'

Primrose turned as red as a raspberry. 'Er . . . I'm afraid I have, your majesty,' she said.

'Oh, how tiresome!' exclaimed the queen. 'I must have a magical person in the castle. I'm afraid, Primrose, that you'll have to go to the Home for Retired Witches, and I'll have to get someone else to take your place.'

Primrose's replacement arrived the very next day, a clever young wizard who had been sent by the Whizz-Kid Employment Agency. He had a brand-new shiny suit-case that was full of all the very latest magical equipment. He made Primrose feel very old-fashioned.

So Primrose sadly packed up her few belongings. Then, after saying goodbye to all her friends at the castle, she flew off on her broomstick to the Home for Retired Witches. She didn't want to go there at all, but she supposed it would be better than spending the night in a haystack.

The Home for Retired Witches was even worse than Primrose had imagined. It was a square, red-brick house with no garden.

And Primrose loved gardens. At the castle, she had often helped the royal gardener tend to the roses.

By the door stood a row of broomsticks. Inside, there were witches everywhere. Most of them were even older than Primrose, and they were all muttering half-remembered magic spells to themselves.

'This is a terrible place,' thought Primrose. 'I don't want to be surrounded by forgetful old witches for the rest of my life. I may be old and forgetful myself, but that doesn't mean I have to spend my life with lots of other old and forgetful people.'

Just as Primrose was thinking of leaving, a bossy-looking matron came up to her and said, 'Ah, you must be Primrose, our new guest. If you would like to park your broomstick outside, I will show you to your room.'

'Er, no thanks, I'm just on a flying visit,' said Primrose, taking off out of the window.

'Phew, that was a narrow

escape,' she thought, zooming up into the clouds. 'And now I must find myself a proper home, although who's going to want to live with an old witch who's forgotten all her magic tricks, I don't know.'

Primrose flew on and on, getting more and more worried. Would she ever find the right home? She

didn't have enough money to stay in a hotel, and what ordinary family would want her? She was just thinking that she might have to spend the rest of her life sleeping in haystacks after all, when she spotted below her the wobbly chimneys of the Old House. 'Now that looks the kind of place that

would put up with an old witch who's forgotten all her magic,' she thought. 'And why, the garden looks like a jungle; I could be of great help there,' and she landed beside the front door.

There she explained to the Old House that she wasn't much use because she had forgotten all her magic, but she was a very good gardener.

The House was delighted to see her. Three visitors were good, four were even better, and he creaked open his front door for her. She flew through it on her broomstick and, inside, came face to face with a monster, a mouse and a ghost.

'Welcome, Primrose,' they all said, and soon made her feel at home.

'A witch now,' whispered the Pink House to the Blue House. 'Well, all I can say is, I hope she turns the house into a frog.'

'Or a worm,' whispered the Blue House.

Hilda Pig

At the very moment that the House, Norman Monster, Nigel Mouse and Gertrude were making Primrose feel at home, a long way away, Hilda Pig was piping cream on to a magnificent chocolate cake.

'It would win a prize,' cried Mr

Brocklebank, the old badger who owned the restaurant. 'Hilda, you are, without a doubt, the best chef in town.'

And he was right, Hilda *was* the best chef in town. People from far and wide came to sample her delicious pies and pastries and chocolate cakes. And they were never disappointed.

Hilda was very, very happy in her job.

And then one day Mr Brocklebank decided it was high time he retired, and so he sold the restaurant to a fox called Mr Fergus Foxglove.

Hilda was very sad to see Mr Brocklebank go, and baked a big

cake, with 'We're going to miss you, Mr B' piped in blue icing on the top.

'I'm going to miss you, too,' said Mr Brocklebank, snuffling into his handkerchief.

Hilda soon discovered that Mr Foxglove didn't like pigs. But the law didn't allow him to sack Hilda, so he tried to make her life as unpleasant as possible, in the hope that she would leave.

'Hilda Pig, you're far too fat,' he would say, curling up his lip to reveal sharp teeth. 'A fat chef is a

very bad advertisement for the restaurant. Why, people might think that if they eat here they will end up the same size as you. Then they won't come here any more and I'll go bankrupt.'

This upset Hilda very much, and so she didn't work as well as she normally did. And every time she did anything even a tiny bit wrong, Mr Foxglove would get very cross.

First she dropped a plate.

'Trust a pig to drop a plate,' Mr Foxglove sneered.

And then some soup boiled over.

'Only a pig could do that,' bellowed Mr Foxglove.

And then Hilda got so flustered that she did something that even now she blushes about whenever she thinks of it. She put salt in the

strawberry pudding and sugar in the Chef's Especially Delicious Beefburgers. They were certainly far from delicious – in fact they were horrible.

'*Ugh*,' said a weasel after taking one bite, and called Mr Foxglove over to complain.

Mr Foxglove apologized to the weasel and rushed into the kitchen.

'You'll be the ruin of me, Hilda Pig,' he shouted, his face even redder than it normally was because he was so angry. But there was also a glint in his eye. This

was the perfect chance to get rid of Hilda.

'You are a stupid fat pig and you can't cook for toffee. I want you out of my kitchen, *now*. And don't you ever show your silly fat pink face in here again.'

'Don't you worry, I *won't*,'

shouted Hilda and, putting her chef's hat and apron into a bag, stumped off.

'I'll easily find another job,' she thought. 'Everyone knows that I'm the best chef in town.'

But what poor Hilda didn't know was that Mr Foxglove had spread unkind rumours about her to the other restaurant owners. He had told them that Hilda, being a pig, smelt like a pigsty, which sometimes made the food taste. He told them that the reason she was so fat was because she ate half the food that was meant for the customers. He also said that no proper restaurant had a girl as a chef. Unfortunately for her, the

restaurant owners believed him.

So when Hilda went to see them to find out whether they needed a chef, they all said, ‘No thank you, Hilda Pig,’ and closed the door.

Hilda tried one restaurant after another, but they all turned her away. When she had tried all the smart restaurants, she tried the less-smart ones. But the very same thing happened. Eventually, she ended up going to the worst café in town. It was called Guzzlers' Café and was owned by a rat called Mr Teeth.

Mr Teeth looked Hilda up and down before wiping tomato sauce from his mouth with his apron. Then, after picking his teeth with the prong of a fork, he said, 'Okay, Hilda Pig, I'll take you on. But you'll have to take off that silly chef's hat – this isn't a posh hotel, you know.'

And it certainly wasn't. For what a terrible mess Hilda found the kitchen in. Grease covered the walls, the cooker looked as though it had had five hundred meals spilt all over it, and the saucepans were caked with stale food.

'I can't work in this mess, Mr Teeth,' said Hilda.

'Well, you'll have to,' growled

Mr Teeth. 'No one's ever complained before.'

And so Hilda had to manage as well as she could.

Very soon she discovered that her job wasn't to cook at all, but to open tins. 'This is no job for the best chef in town,' she thought sadly as she emptied baked beans on to a plate.

Hilda began to get really fed-up, and when she found an army of maggots feasting on some rotten meat in the larder, she decided that it was high time to leave. So she did.

'Surely I can find someone who would appreciate good cooking,' she thought as she waddled along the road.

Suddenly, she smelt food burning. She looked to see where the smell was coming from. She peered through rusty gates at a

garden that was like a jungle and saw, outside a big dark house, a witch running along with a frying pan that had flames coming out of it.

'I think I might be needed there,' Hilda thought, and walked through the squeaking gates and up the overgrown path.

Hilda explained to the House

that she was a chef and the House said, 'We could really do with a chef. Welcome.' He was delighted to have another visitor. Four visitors were good, five were even better, and he creaked open the front door for her.

Hilda walked in. She introduced herself to the others, who were all sitting round the fire.

Everyone made her feel at home. 'I'm so pleased you've come,' said Primrose. 'Now I won't have to do any more cooking – or, rather, burning!'

The Pink House and the Blue House looked at each other.

'The next thing you know, it'll be a pigsty,' said the Pink House. 'And you know what they smell like.'

Father Christmas

At the very moment that the House, Norman Monster, Nigel Mouse, Gertrude Ghost and Primrose Witch were making Hilda feel at home, a long, long way away, in a freezing-cold

castle at the top of an icy mountain, Father Christmas slammed down his cup of tea into the saucer and said, 'Oh, blithering snowstorms!'

'What's wrong *this* time?' sighed Julian, the reindeer, who was filing his toe nails.

'My cup of tea has frozen solid,' said Father Christmas. 'Look,'

and he turned the cup upside-down. He was right. It had frozen solid. 'Honestly,' said Father Christmas, 'I could cry. Except that there would be no point. The tears would turn to icicles before they'd even left my eyes. Why, my blood will freeze next. And then you'll have a frozen-solid Father Christmas on your hands.'

'Oh, *do* stop moaning,' said Julian, polishing his antlers with a duster. 'Really, anyone would think we were in the Arctic Circle.'

'We are – practically,' said Father Christmas, breathing on his red hands. The cold air made his breath look like steam from a train. 'I mean, just look at the

ceiling. It's covered in icicles. This climate is fit for neither man nor beast – and certainly not elderly Father Christmases.'

'Speak for yourself,' said Julian. 'It suits me well enough. You ought to grow yourself a fur coat. Then you'd be lovely and warm, like me.'

'Very funny,' said Father Christmas crossly, and returned to making his toys, although his fingers were so numb they could hardly move. He sighed. The thought of spending the rest of his life living in a freezing cold castle in Greenland with only a bad-tempered, vain reindeer for company, was not a pleasant one. 'What I'd love to do is live in a nice warm house with nice interesting people,' he thought.

The one thing that was cheering up Father Christmas slightly was the fact that tomorrow was Christmas Eve, which meant that while he was delivering the presents he might manage to get

warmed up in the children's houses before spending another cold, shivery year in Greenland.

But he was worried that Julian might have a tantrum, the way he often did on Christmas Eve. One year he'd refused to pull the sleigh at all, saying that it was bad for his health, and so, at the last minute, Father Christmas had to find another reindeer.

'I hope you aren't going to throw a tantrum, this year, Julian,' said Father Christmas.

'Actually, I was thinking about having one,' said Julian, studying his face in the mirror. 'All my friends are going to a party on Christmas Eve, and I'd rather like to go.'

'You can go after we've delivered the presents,' Father Christmas told him firmly.

While Father Christmas stayed up all night finishing the toys, Julian went off ice-skating with his friends. By the next day, all the toys were ready. Father Christmas loaded them up into a large sack and put it in the sleigh. Then he combed his long white beard, polished his black boots and put on his smartest red outfit. Mean-

while, Julian was giving his antlers a final polish and his coat a final brush, grumbling all the time.

Father Christmas harnessed him to the sleigh and then they were off, flying through the starry sky.

'I wish you'd go on a diet. You weigh a tonne,' grumbled Julian.

Eventually, they reached the first house and landed on the roof. Father Christmas selected some toys and climbed down the chimney.

'I hope you get stuck,' muttered Julian rudely. Luckily, Father Christmas didn't hear.

And so, for the next three hours, Father Christmas climbed up and

down chimneys, while Julian waited for him on the rooftops, stamping his hoof and getting more and more impatient. 'The party will be finished by the time I get back,' he thought crossly.

Though Father Christmas was getting quite warm climbing up and down chimneys, he longed to get *really* warm. But as yet he hadn't found one house that had a fire burning. 'How I'd love to sit by one just for a few minutes to warm up my old bones before setting off back to that freezing castle. Oh, well, I'll just have to do without,' he thought sadly as he climbed up the last chimney.

He got into the sleigh, and was just about to say, 'Let's go home, Julian,' when he spotted, through some trees, a tall wobbly chimney. And out of the chimney came smoke!

'Er, Julian,' said Father Christmas. 'We have just one more call to make, over there,' and he pointed to the chimney.

'Oh, honestly,' said Julian, setting off. 'I know why you want to go there – because it's got a fire. No children live there, you know. Just look at the place. It's a shambles. I'm going to go straight through the roof if I'm not careful.'

'I won't be long,' said Father Christmas, climbing out of the sleigh. Taking a deep breath, he clambered into the smoke-filled chimney.

'You'd better not be,' said Julian. 'Or I'll miss my party. If you aren't back in five minutes I'll go without you.'

'Don't you dare,' shouted Father Christmas. Suddenly he was falling . . . and then landing – crunch! – in the glowing embers of the fire. How good it felt to be really warm at last. But soon he felt a bit too warm, so he jumped out on to the hearth just as his red trousers were about to go up in flames.

Suddenly, Father Christmas was aware that he wasn't alone in the room. He looked round and saw what seemed like a whole crowd of people, animals, monsters and ghosts. His mouth dropped open, then, 'Thundering icicles!' he exclaimed. 'I hope I'm not intruding on your little party.'

'Not at all,' growled Norman Monster. 'We're always pleased to have visitors.'

The House agreed. Five visitors were good, six were even better.

'I say,' said Father Christmas. 'What a bit of luck. I have exactly six presents left, and there are six of you, including the House.' And

he fished in his sack and pulled out a small framed picture for the House, a red handkerchief for Primrose Witch, a white handkerchief for Gertrude Ghost, a rolling pin for Hilda Pig, a box of paints for Nigel Mouse and another book of jokes for Norman Monster.

'What perfect presents,' they all said. 'Thank you, Father Christmas.'

'A pleasure,' said Father Christmas. 'The very least I can do after you've so kindly let me sit by your lovely warm fire.'

Then the House said, 'Would you like to make your home here? There is just one spare bedroom left.'

'Oh, please do,' cried Primrose.

'You could borrow my broomstick to deliver the presents.'

'Well,' said Father Christmas. 'As much as I'd like to, my reindeer is waiting for me on the roof. Goodbye everybody. Happy Christmas,' and, now nice and warm, he climbed back up the chimney.

Everyone was very sad to see him go. But, two minutes later, he was back again!

'Blithering snowstorms!' exclaimed Father Christmas. 'My tiresome reindeer has gone without me. So I was wondering – er – if I could take you up on your kind offer to stay, after all.'

'Hurray!' everyone shouted. 'You're most welcome, Father Christmas.'

'Ah,' sighed the House happily. 'I'm full again at last.'

The Pink House and the Blue House said nothing. Father Christmas hadn't been to visit them, because the children who lived in them had gone away for Christmas, and so they were all dark and shut up. For the first time, they began to feel a little bit jealous of the Old House.

'Never mind,' whispered the Pink House. 'It's going to be pulled down by the men from the Council soon.'

'Thank goodness for that,' said the Blue House. 'That house is really beginning to get on my nerves.'

Christmas Day

Everyone had a lovely Christmas Day. It had been snowing during the night, and so the garden had turned into a white jungle.

'Let's build a snow mouse,' cried Nigel and so they did, apart from Father Christmas, who dozed happily by the fire.

For lunch they had carrot soup (they'd found the carrots growing in the garden), made by Hilda, which tasted almost as good as roast turkey. Everyone wore brightly coloured paper hats that Nigel had made. They sang carols, and Norman Monster read some jokes out of his Monster Joke Book. It was just like a proper Christmas.

Then, as it grew dark outside and the snowflakes fell gently against the window-panes, they sat round the fire and each in turn recounted their adventures which had caused them to end up at the Old House.

They heard about Norman's nagging mother and father, and how he left home to seek his fortune. They heard about how Wilf Whiskers had made Nigel's life such a misery that he had to look for a new home. They heard about how Gertrude played tricks on the duchess and about her difficulties in finding a suitable house to

haunt. They heard about how Primrose forgot all her magic spells. They heard about how Hilda was sacked by Mr Foxglove, and about Mr Teeth and the Guzzlers' Café. And, finally, they heard about Father Christmas sitting in his freezing-cold castle, arguing all day with his reindeer.

'And so here we all are, living together,' said Primrose. 'Now tell us about your past, House.'

'Well,' said the House. 'I was designed – ooh, over a hundred years ago – by a young man called John Wilkinson. He was soon to be married to a beautiful girl called Sarah. Because Sarah had lived in a small, tumbledown cottage all her life, John wanted her to have the finest, grandest house in the area. And I was! You should have seen me then. I had shining white paint, white pillars and a brass door knocker which was polished every day by the maid. And you should have seen my garden – sweeping lawns and rose bushes, and even a pond with a fountain in the middle. Often, John and Sarah would hold grand balls in me, to

which women in beautiful gowns and men in curly white wigs came.' The House paused. Tears had appeared in his upstairs windows. Then he continued, 'John and Sarah had three children, a boy and two girls. They would spend hours sliding down my banisters and playing hide and seek in my attics. Those were the days,' sighed the House, and the others sighed, too. How lovely it all sounded.

'For many years, I was the happiest house in the world – I was loved and cared for and filled with laughter. I should have known it was too good to last. The years passed and John, now an old man, became ill and died; Sarah died soon afterwards, of a broken heart. The two girls got married and moved far away, and so Albert, their son, took me over. That

was the start of my downfall. For all Albert cared about was betting, and he lost all his money. He neglected me: when tiles fell off my roof, he didn't bother to replace them; when my paint began to flake, he ignored it. Gradually, I began to crumble and decay and, by the time Albert died, no one wanted to live in me – not even a

spider. And so there I was, lonely and miserable and rotting away – and then you all came along, and now I'm full again. Thank you – all of you – for coming here and making an old tumbledown house very happy.'

'Thank *you* for giving us all somewhere to live,' said Hilda. 'Without you we would all be

sleeping in haystacks. And now, what I suggest is we all set to work to get you back to how you were when you were new.'

Everyone agreed.

'We'll give you lots of coats of lovely white paint,' said Nigel.

'And we'll have your garden back to looking how it used to look, with sweeping lawns and rose bushes, in no time at all,' said Primrose.

'And we'll paint all your rooms and then we'll hold grand balls,' said Gertrude.

'Do you think a white curly wig would suit me?' asked Norman Monster, and everybody laughed.

They continued to talk about what they would do to the House in order to return him to his former glory.

But the House was growing more and more uncomfortable. Then he took a deep breath and said, 'I'm afraid that I've got some bad news for you all. I should have told you when you first arrived, but I didn't want to put you off living here. The fact is . . .' He paused. 'The fact is, I'm going to be pulled down soon by the men from the Council.'

'Blithering icicles!' exclaimed Father Christmas and then, for a whole minute, apart from the snowflakes patting gently against the window-panes and the crackle of the fire, there was silence.

They couldn't believe it. They'd just found the perfect home, and

now it was going to be pulled down. Having to look for somewhere else to live was too terrible to think about.

Suddenly, Gertrude said, 'Well, we shall just have to stop them.'

'But how?' said Nigel, his whiskers all a-twitch. 'They will be big tough men and they will have dynamite and pickaxes.'

Everyone looked at Gertrude.

'Don't worry,' she said. 'I've got it all planned. This is what we've got to do . . .'

Bill and Bert

One morning soon after Christmas, two men called Bill and Bert pushed a cart up to the rusty gates of the Old House. In the cart were pickaxes, iron balls attached to chains, and dynamite.

Bill and Bert peered through the rusty gates and past the garden

that looked more like a jungle than a garden, and saw the Old House.

'Doesn't it look spooky, Bert,' said Bill.

'Yes it does, Bill,' said Bert. 'And it's certainly in a very sorry state. It won't take us any time at all to pull it down.'

'No, it won't,' said Bill. 'I reckon, Bert, that in an hour or so's time we will be sitting in the Goat and Fox drinking ale.'

'Righto, Bill,' said Bert. 'We'd better get started, then.'

So they pushed the cart through the squeaking gates and up the overgrown path.

Suddenly, they stopped dead in their tracks. For they had caught sight of a large sign nailed to the trunk of a tree. A skull and cross-bones was painted on it and, underneath, it said 'PLAGUE. KEEP OUT.'

'Jumping gerbils, Bill,' said Bert. 'I don't want to catch the plague, thank you very much. Let's get out of here.'

'Don't be daft, Bert,' said Bill. 'No one lives in the house, there-

fore there's no one to catch the plague from. Anyway, that sign's probably been up there for years.'

'It looks like fresh paint to me,' muttered Bill.

Nigel Mouse, hiding behind the tree, had his handkerchief stuffed into his mouth to stop himself from laughing.

'Oh, come on Bill,' said Bert. 'The sooner we get this house

pulled down, the sooner we can go for a drink at the Goat and Fox.'

And so they began to walk a little further up the path.

Suddenly, they stopped dead in their tracks again.

'Well I never, Bert,' said Bill. 'If that isn't Father Christmas, my name isn't Bill Jones.'

'Jumping gerbils, you're right Bill,' said Bert, scratching his head. 'I've always wanted to meet Father Christmas. I wonder if he'd give me his autograph.'

Bill nudged Bert to shut up. Father Christmas was coming over to them. He looked very cross.

'Will you chaps please get off my land,' he ordered.

'I'm afraid we can't, Sir,' said Bert. 'You see we've come to pull your house down. Council's orders.'

'Pull my house down! But that's *outrageous*,' bellowed Father Christmas. 'You can't pull my house down when I'm living in it.'

'I'm afraid orders are orders, Sir,' said Bill and took a few steps forward.

And then several things happened at once. Later, when Bill and Bert told their friends about it at the Goat and Fox, they couldn't remember exactly what they saw first – a fat pig waving a

rolling pin, a witch on a broomstick, or a ghost.

'Jumping gerbils, Bill,' said Bert, turning white. 'Am I dreaming or can I really see a pig with a rolling pin, a witch on a broomstick, and a ghost coming towards us?'

'No, you're not dreaming,' said Bert. 'Unless we're both having the same dream, and that's not very likely. Ouch!' For Hilda had started hitting him with the rolling

pin. And then Primrose flew straight at them and, with the end of her broomstick, knocked their caps clean off their heads.

'She could turn us into toads at any minute, Bill,' said Bert through chattering teeth.

Meanwhile, Gertrude was floating nearer and nearer. 'This is the creepiest house I've ever been to, Bert,' said Bill. 'Let's get out of here.'

And, just as they were about to run away, they saw the most terrifying sight of all. For thundering towards them, causing the ground to shake, was the biggest, ugliest, most hideous monster Bill and Bert had ever seen.

'EEK!' cried Bert.

'Run for it, Bert,' cried Bill, and, without looking back, they ran as fast as their legs would carry them towards the rusty gates.

Soon, everyone in the Goat and Fox and at the Council offices and, in fact, everyone in the town, had heard the story about Bill and Bert and the haunted house full of monsters and ghosts and witches, not to mention a big strong pig and a cross Father Christmas, all of whom had the plague.

'I wouldn't go back there for all the tea in China,' said Bert. 'Would you, Bill?'

'Not for all the coffee in Brazil, Bert,' said Bill.

They told this to the man from the Council, for whom they worked.

'Well, I'm not going there, either,' said their boss. 'And so the House had better stay put, after all.'

Meanwhile, back in the House, everyone was dancing with glee. It had worked! Their home had been saved.

'And now we must set to work

putting you to rights, House,' said Father Christmas.

First, Primrose – for, without her broomstick and black hat, she looked the most normal of any of them – was sent to the shops with Norman's twelve crowns. She came back laden with paint and tools and groceries. Then they set

to work. Primrose flew round the house on her broomstick, sweeping away the cobwebs. Gertrude dusted and polished with her white robe and Nigel began to paint the walls. Norman, because he was so strong, carted bricks and repaired walls and staircases; and

Father Christmas, because he knew how to make toy furniture, began to make proper furniture. Hilda scrubbed floors and kept them all going with her delicious soups. Everyone worked very, very hard.

But Hilda started to get worried. They couldn't eat soups for ever and, besides, the vegetables in the garden would run out, sooner or later. During a tea break she told the others how worried she was, and they said they were worried, too. There was still so much to be done, and they were

fast running out of paint and nails and other vital things – and all of Norman's crowns had been spent.

'What we need is money,' said Nigel, his whiskers twitching.

'I wonder if there's any treasure buried in the garden,' said Gertrude.

'No there isn't,' said the House gloomily.

They looked at each other. Whatever could they do? 'Perhaps we'll all starve to death,' said Nigel.

Suddenly, they heard an almighty sneeze – **A-TISHOO.** It was so loud that the whole House shook. 'Primrose must have got some dust up her nose,' they laughed, and went back to thinking about where they could get some money.

A few minutes later, Primrose flew into the kitchen on her broomstick. She was looking as pleased as if she'd just found a thousand crowns! 'Guess what,' she cried. 'I expect you heard me sneeze just now . . .'

'We were almost deafened by it,' laughed Norman.

'Well,' said Primrose. 'After I'd recovered from it I felt sort of – well, very odd. And then I realized what had happened: the sneeze had jogged my memory. And I can now remember my magic spells! Which means that I can magic up practically anything we need. All our problems are over!'

A few days later, the House was back to how it had been over a hundred years ago. It was gleaming white, had pillars and a sparkling brass door knob, sweeping lawns and even a pond with a fountain. Indoors there were vases of flowers in every room, and beautiful furniture.

They had a great big party to

celebrate. Hilda, with the help of Primrose's magic, cooked pies and pastries and a magnificent chocolate cake with 'Home Sweet Home' piped on top. They drank champagne, Primrose and Hilda danced on the table, Father Christmas and Gertrude sang some songs, Norman told jokes, and Nigel did conjuring tricks.

Everyone had a great time – except for the Blue House and the Pink House. They felt very jealous. Their owners hardly ever seemed to enjoy themselves these days. And, beside the new Old House, they looked very old and shabby. Never again were they

unkind to him. In fact, they were always extremely polite.

So Norman Monster, Nigel Mouse, Gertrude Ghost, Primrose Witch, Hilda Pig and Father Christmas all lived happily ever after. And the new Old House was the happiest of all.

Thanks to one of Primrose's magic spells, they are all alive to this very day and so, if you pass a freshly painted white house where an ugly monster is telling jokes, a ghost is somersaulting across the lawn, a mouse is painting a picture, a fat pig is sampling her cooking, Father Christmas is making toys in the warm sun and a witch is doing a spot of gardening, why don't you give them a wave?